Weird, wild, and wonderful

Crabs

By Kerry Nagle

Gareth Stevens
Publishing

Please visit our Web site **www.garethstevens.com**. For a free color catalog of all our high-quality books, call toll free 1-800-542-2595 or fax 1-877-542-2596.

Library of Congress Cataloging-in-Publication Data
Nagle, Kerry.
Crabs / Kerry Nagle.
    p. cm. -- (Weird, wild, and wonderful)
Includes index.
ISBN 978-1-4339-3574-9 (library binding)
1. Crabs--Juvenile literature. I. Title.
QL444.M33N34 2010
595.3'86--dc22
                                    2009043974

Published in 2010 by
Gareth Stevens Publishing
111 East 14th Street, Suite 349
New York, NY 10003

For Gareth Stevens Publishing:
Art Direction: Haley Harasymiw
Editorial Direction: Kerri O'Donnell

Designed in Australia by www.design-ed.com.au

Photography by Kathie Atkinson
Additional photographs: Tim Hellier/imagequestmarine.com, p. 7a; © James Wood, p. 11c; Jim Greenfield/imagequestmarine.com, p. 15a; Photolibrary, p. 17b.

Printed in the United States of America

CPSIA compliance information: Batch #CW10GS: For further information contact Gareth Stevens, New York, New York, at 1-800-542-2595.

Contents

What Are Crabs?

What has ten limbs, eyes on **stalks**, and walks sideways? A crab!

Most wild crabs live in the sea. Some, though, live on the land. They come in different shapes and sizes. But crabs have some things in common. They have a hard, outer shell that is a bit like **armor**. The shell is called a **carapace**. It **protects** their soft body. Crabs do not have a backbone.

This crab lives in the ocean. Its back legs are shaped like paddles. This helps it swim.

Crabs **shed their shells** as they get bigger. It takes a few days for a new shell to grow.

Crabs have five pairs of legs. The first two legs are claws. They are called **pincers** or **chelipeds**. They can give you a nasty nip!

The claws are very useful. They hold and carry food. They dig into sand and mud. They can crack open shells. They can even scare off enemies.

A crab's two eyes are on stalks that poke up. They can move them up and down.

A crab's eyes work a bit like a periscope. They can look in all different directions.

Have you ever seen patterns like this on the beach? They are made by the sand bubbler crab.

Fact Bite

Watch out for sand crabs at the beach. They might give you a bite on the toe if they feel scared!

5

New Life

Male crabs have to attract females to **mate**. Some male crabs beat a claw on the ground. Others wave a claw in a wild way. One type of crab does a dance. He stands on the tips of his walking legs. He then uses his swimming legs to rock from side to side.

The male fiddler crab waves his large claw at the female. He wants her to choose him as a **mate**.

Fact Bite

Female crabs keep their eggs healthy by washing water over them.

Female crabs lay a large number of eggs at one time. Some lay as many as one million eggs! The eggs are carried around by the female on her **abdomen**.

Young crabs **hatch** from the eggs. At first, they are tiny **larvae**. They look weird—not like adult crabs at all. The female sends the larvae into the sea. Here, they drift around as they grow. The young crabs shed their skin many times before they are adults.

This crab larva has just hatched from an egg.

Female crabs carry their eggs in a flap below the abdomen. This female crab is waving her legs to defend herself.

7

What Do Crabs Eat?

While crabs are busy feeding, they must watch out for danger. This crab went too close to an octopus. It ended up as dinner!

Different types of crabs eat different types of food. Some eat plants. They are called herbivores. Some are carnivores. That means they eat meat. They feed on snails, worms, and small fish. Some crabs eat plants and meat. They are omnivores.

Fact Bite

Some crabs find their food in mud and sand. They take in a mouthful and spit out the bits that they don't want.

This crab is eating a seabird that has died.

Some crabs will eat anything they find in the wild. They will even eat things that are dead and rotting. They are called **scavengers**.

Crabs use their pincers to catch and hold their food. These claws are very strong. They can even crack open snail shells. The crab pulls out the snail's soft body to eat it.

Algae make a tasty meal for this crab.

Can You See Me?

Look carefully at this photograph. Can you see the crab? Its color helps it hide from its enemies.

Life in the wild is full of danger for crabs. Many other creatures like to eat them. Crabs make tasty meals for fish, birds, seals, turtles, octopuses— and humans!

Crabs use tricks to hide themselves from animals who want to eat them.

This little crab is hiding in some soft coral. Its body and claws match the shape and color of the coral.

Some crabs hide under rocks and in holes. Others bury themselves in the sand. Others are the same color as their surroundings.

Some crabs dress up to hide themselves. The seaweed decorator crab covers itself with seaweed. It cuts off a piece of seaweed with its claws. Then it sticks the seaweed onto its shell. Special hairs on its back are shaped like hooks. These hairs act like Velcro. They hold the decorations in place.

This tiny sponge crab is in disguise! It is wearing a cap of purple sponge. This helps it blend in with the sponge on the rock.

This crab has covered itself with seaweed.

If it stays still, this rock crab is hard to see.

Who Stole My Shell?

The hermit crab has no shell of its own. It just has a soft body. To protect itself, it wears an empty shell. These have usually been left behind by snails.

Hermit crabs hatch from eggs in the sea. They live in the sea for the first part of their life. They breathe through **gills**. As they grow, they change. Their gills change, too. Now they can breathe air. When they are about 0.2 inch (5 mm) wide, they move onto land.

Fact Bite

Hermit crabs live on land and in the sea.

Two hermit crabs

Most hermit crabs are scavengers. They will eat rotting plants or dead animals. They might also feed on live **prey**—even other crabs.

The hermit crab's first two legs are different sizes. The large one makes a "door" to the crab's shell. The crab pulls its body up inside the shell. It uses the large claw to close the shell's opening.

The red hermit crab has hairy red legs with white spots.

This hermit crab has lost its shell. It is in danger of being eaten while it is homeless.

13

Moving House

Hermit crabs are wonderful house-hunters. They will spend a long time choosing a shell to live in. Different shells will be "tried on for size." The one that fits best becomes the crab's new home.

As the crab grows, it gets too big for its shell. Then it's time to move out. The hermit crab must look for a bigger shell.

First, the crab moves next to its new home. It climbs out of its old shell.

The crab carefully moves across to the new shell.

It can be hard to find a good shell. Hermit crabs sometimes have wild fights over a shell. Some crabs will even steal another crab's shell.

Some hermit crabs carry a "housemate" on their shell. **Sea anemones** grab on to the crab's shell and make it their home. The anemones hide the crabs. Their stinging **tentacles** scare off the crab's enemies. When the crab changes shells, it often takes its anemone with it!

Fact Bite

If a hermit crab can't find a shell to move in to, it might cover itself with bits of plants, such as a coconut shell.

The crab climbs backwards into its new home.

15

Life on Land

Fact Bite

Some crabs live on the land, away from the sea. Adult crabs visit the sea when it is time to **breed**. The young crabs grow in the sea. When they are big enough, they move to land.

The largest land crab is the coconut crab. It can climb trees. It is so strong it can crack open coconuts!

Land crabs are nocturnal. This means they are active during the night. That's when they look for food. Many land crabs live on **tropical islands**. It can get very hot during the day. The crabs need to find somewhere cool to rest. Old turtle shells or bush branches are wonderful shady spots.

These hermit crabs rest under branches during the day.

This old turtle shell shades these hermit crabs. Late in the day, when it is cooler, the crabs come out. That's when they look for food.

These red crabs are on their long trek to the sea. They will cross roads and climb stairs in their journey.

Red crabs live on Christmas Island. They dig **burrows** to get away from the heat. Every year, millions of these crabs go down to the sea to breed. They all go at the same time. The crabs will walk up to 5 miles (8 km) in five days. It looks like some weird parade.

17

Big Claws

The male fiddler crab is easy to spot. It has one large, orange claw. This claw looks odd because it is so much bigger than the other claw.

These big claws are very useful. Males like to show them off to female fiddler crabs. They wave them in the air and tap them on the ground. That is how a male says "Look at me. I'd be a wonderful mate."

A male fiddler crab has one large, orange claw.

Fact Bite

The fiddler crab gets its name from how its claws look. The big one looks like a violin. (A violin is also called a fiddle.) The small one looks like the violin bow.

The large claw is also a weapon. Male fiddler crabs have wild battles with each other. They will fight over food.

Sometimes, a male might lose his large claw. If this happens, the small claw gets bigger. A new, small claw will grow to replace the lost claw.

This male crab is trying to **impress** a female with its large, orange claw.

Two fiddler crabs fighting

19

Safety in Numbers

Soldier crabs are not like other crabs. They walk forwards, not sideways. They are called soldier crabs because they gather in great "armies." The large numbers help them keep safe from animals that want to eat them.

Soldier crabs live in **estuaries**. These are places where a river meets the sea. At high tide, water covers the ground. Soldier crabs don't have gills, so they can't breathe underwater. They need to stay in holes they dig in the ground. These holes have air for them to breathe. The crabs plug up the holes with sand. This keeps the water out.

An "army" of soldier crabs comes up to feed when the tide goes out.

At low tide, the ground is no longer covered with water. The soldier crabs now come out to feed. Huge numbers appear all at once. It is a weird sight!

To feed, the soldier crab rolls sand into little balls. It sorts through the sand for food to eat.

If they get scared, soldier crabs can disappear fast. They twist into the ground like a corkscrew.

These two soldier crabs are fighting. They both want the same territory.

The soldier crab's legs have joints.

Fact Bite

The soldier crab has a round, blue body. It is about the size of a nickel. Its legs are long with purple stripes.

Fact File: Crab Features

Crabs live in many different places. Some of them have special claws or legs.

Crab Features		
Type	**Main habitat**	**Special claws or legs**
sand crab	shallow water off sandy beaches	fourth legs shaped like paddles for swimming
hermit crab	many different **habitats** on land and sea	one larger claw for protection and for sealing off its shell
red crab	rain forest	claws are the same size
fiddler crab	near water on mud or sand	one large, orange claw; one much smaller claw
soldier crab	mangroves, beaches, and estuaries	legs that walk forward, not sideways
coconut crab	sandy beaches, coastal areas	very strong claws; legs good for climbing

Glossary

abdomen   the lower part of an animal's body

algae   very small plants that grow in or near water

armor   strong covering that protects the body

breed   make babies

burrows   holes in the ground dug by an animal

carapace   a hard shell that covers an animal

chelipeds   the first pair of legs that have the claws

disguise   something that changes the way you look

estuaries   places where the mouth of a river meets the sea

gills   body parts for breathing underwater

habitats   natural places where animals or plants usually live

hatch   to break out of an egg

impress   to gain attention or interest

larvae   newly hatched young that are not fully developed and don't look like the adults

mate (a)   an animal's partner in making babies

mate (to)   what two animals do to make babies

periscope   a tool for looking in places that are hard to see

pincers   curved claws

prey   an animal that is hunted and killed for food

protects   keeps safe

scavengers   animals or birds that feed on dead animals that they find

sea anemones   sea animals with stinging tentacles around the mouth

shed   to get rid of

stalks   narrow stems that hold up the eyes

tentacles   long, thin body parts that grab or feel things

tropical islands   islands near the equator that are hot and humid

For Further Information

Books

Gilpin, Daniel. *Lobsters, Crabs, and Other Crustaceans.* Mankato, MN: Compass Point Books, 2006.

Rhodes, Mary Jo, and David Hall. *Crabs (Undersea Encounters).* Danbury, CT: Childrens Press, 2007.

Web Sites

Crabs
http://www.cyhaus.com/marine/crabs.htm

KidsKonnect.com
http://www.kidskonnect.com/subject-index/13-animals/24-crabs.html

Publisher's note to educators and parents: Our editors have carefully reviewed these Web sites to ensure that they are suitable for students. Many Web sites change frequently, however, and we cannot guarantee that a site's future contents will continue to meet our high standards of quality and educational value. Be advised that students should be closely supervised whenever they access the Internet.

Index